Woman Song

for better and for worse

JUNE COMARSH GILLAM

Publisher: Gorilla Girl Ink
Website: www.gorillagirlpress.com
Email: gorillagirlink@gmail.com
Auburn, California
Copyright © 2018 June Gillam
All rights reserved.

ISBN: 978-0-9858838-9-8
Library of Congress Control Number: 2018905124

Published in other venues
Pride, *Enclave*, Napa College, 1980
In Gratitude Thursday, *From the Mud to the Pie*, Vol. 1, 1980
Woman Song, *Butterfly Tree*, Vol. 1, 1982
Solstices, *Writing for our Lives*, Vol. 7, 2, 1999
The Coming Dust, *Wild Edges*, Vol. 6, 2010
Shameless Hussy Looks Back, *Peregrine*, Vol. 28, 2015

DEDICATION

Dedicated to my friends over all these years and fears and tears, along with the laughter and the songs. And to the readers who relish these poems.

You know who you are.

Table of Contents

- WHAT'S IN A WOMAN'S NAME? ... i
- WOMAN SONG ... 1
- ANOTHER UNEMPLOYED HOUSEWIFE ... 3
- TO MY NEXT HUSBAND ... 6
- BUTTERBALL ... 7
- PROFESSIONAL ... 8
- GAMBIT ... 9
- BODYSMITHING ... 10
- SHOPPING SPREE ... 11
- IN GRATITUDE THURSDAY ... 12
- MEMENTO ... 13
- CULINARY SPECULATIONS ... 14
- FAMILY GAME ... 15
- EARTHMOTHERS RISING ... 16
- IN THE DAYS BEFORE GLASS CEILINGS ... 18
- SERVICE STATION ... 19
- CHIAROSCURO ... 20
- PRIDE ... 21
- FRIENDS ... 22
- FOR SELECTRIC EARS ... 23
- STUFFED ... 24
- SOFA TRAP ... 25

EXISTENTIAL ANXIETY	26
BEGIN AGAIN	27
READING MATTER	28
SOLITARY	29
LABELS	30
SOLSTICES	31
THE COMING DUST	32
SHAMELESS HUSSY LOOKS BACK	33
@Online Dating	36
SUNSET SONG	37
WOMAN SONG MUSIC	39
ABOUT THE AUTHOR	41
Other books by June Gillam	43
Other books published by Gorilla Girl Ink	44

WHAT'S IN A WOMAN'S NAME?

Back and back. Last names. Men's names. I've collected a string of them, some Welsh, some Czechoslovakian, some English, some Latvian, some German. I could make a necklace of them and wear it around town, but instead I've put six of them on my Facebook page.

Last week a friend asked why I had so many names. Marriages to three men, I said, but even my original last name was Daddy man's name, a hearty blustery hunting man, a charming business man, a Skalisky man, one of nine boys and three girls born to Skalisky grandfather man back in frigid Minnesota. Grandfather man's wife, Grandma Nettie, explained she had so many children because she was hard of hearing. Every night when they got into bed, grandpa man would ask her if she wanted to go to sleep or what. She would holler, "What?"

So Bohemian men they were but my mother's father man was Tom Price. Price. Ap Rhys. Welsh for son of Rhys. Never heard of anyone named for being daughter of Rhys. Dot. Daughter of. DotRhys. Dryes? Tries?

Mother's mother's last name was Hubbard, then Osborn after Hubbard died. English names.

My first last name change came with husband number one—Kimmel, German, sounds like the liquor Kummel, Kimmels don't swear, Kimmels don't smoke, said my Kimmelman. Kimmels belong to country clubs and keep their houses well tended, entertain with aplomb, stay married.

So then came second last name change, to Comarsh, which was the term for the drunken party at the end of the college year in Latvia. Forgot to ask if that was true when I was there in that lovely country which won its independence from the Soviet Union with a bloodless singing revolution. Comarsh was a wonderful singer, played the guitar, too, a cricket on the hearth who jumped onto a sailing ship and departed. My poetry began to be published under that name.

Finally there was the final last name change-Gillam, the name of the bread Lady Gregory served the Abbey Theater players in Dublin, Gillam—sustenance, dependable, delicious, sacramental. His ashes rest now in Trinity Cathedral Columbarium; here lie the end of my last names.

<u>First names though, women's names.</u> June. I was born in June but due in July and named after a friend of my mother—a young neighbor, June. My mother knew three Junes, but I've rarely met one, and when I do, I feel a bit offended as if they've taken something belonging to me. Eleanor belonged to one of my father's three sisters and one of my mother's three sisters, as well, so June Eleanor it was, though I hated that name when I was young and pretended it was Ellie. Now I love it for the aunties and Eleanor Roosevelt, as well.

Augusta, my great grandmother's middle name—Nancy Augusta. Then to find Lady Augusta in Ireland who started the Abbey Theater with Yeats—what a joy. So yes, some men's and some women's names—June Eleanor Skalisky Kimmel Comarsh Augusta Gillam-- too many to fit on the tiny columbarium brass name plate in Sacramento's Trinity Cathedral that's already paid for. I guess I can never die.

WOMAN SONG

ONE
And she had a little
mocha
heart-shaped
birthmark

nestled in the curve
of her calf

and she noticed
he never noticed
and she loved it
just the same.

TWO
And she had a
string of stretch marks
on her belly

mapping
their growing
babies

and she noticed
he never noticed
and she loved them
just the same.

THREE
And she had a
set of wrinkles
on her forehead

from fretting as he grew old

and she noticed
he never noticed
and she loved them
just the same.

FOUR
And she wore a
shock of white hair

on top of her head
like a crown

and she noticed
he couldn't notice
and she loved it
just the same.

For guitar chords for this song, see Woman Song Music, p. 39 and June Gillam's YouTube channel.

ANOTHER UNEMPLOYED HOUSEWIFE

The red fat-vested
Ringling Brothers agent
Slides sausage fingers
Down gold chain and
Slips out a round watch
Ticking.

"Time for a side show interview!"
he booms, tickings and boomings
curl up the tips of his thin black mustache.
"We're always in the market for bona-fide freaks!"
he barks at the one lone applicant
approaching the personnel office.

"Slip right over the window ledge,
slide on through this generous opening
I've left for you at the bottom.
That's a good girl, legs first,
You won't fall!"

She scrapes feet and butt and backbone in
But that jutting jaw won't let
Her pass all the way on through.

"Here, here, we'll help!"
shriek professional freaks clustered inside.

Reptile man cradles her calloused feet,
Bearded Bernice shoulders her stretch-marked hips
And winks at two-headed Harry
Resting her waist in his neck fork.
They support her

Like Beautyrest coils
Covered in ticking.

The agent glows directing such a show.
"And now your head,
turn it sideways, dear,
or you'll never get it through—
that jaw gets in your way!
You'll see I'm right
If you just adjust your inclination
One more time."

Obedient, she glides right in,
Lands on her feet
And pirouettes to display
Her resume-splattered apron
To best advantage.
With white bone fingertips
She lightly tosses salad days.

The agents black brows furrow
Toward his bulbous nose
He checks his gold watch
Ticking all the time.

She extends her wedding-banded hand
Shaking salt and pepper onto the
Wounded port roast.
Hold the poem!
Roast in the racked pan.
Wiping bloody drainboards
With greasy spiced hands
She answers the lifeline
That rings over – hello?
And sinks her own –goodbye!
Where's a pencil?
Time to pop another
Pork roast in the oven.

Woman Song

The red-vested agent frowns again and asks
"What's so unusual about you?
You look like a perfectly normal housewife."

She displays her green cunt singing
"Nobody does it better," in a stranger's voice.
She unveils her neon womb flashing the red
ONE MORE TRY FOR A BOY sign.
She points to the forked tongue
Rolling in her mealy mouth:
"Yes, dear, Get the camera, get the sports car,
sailboat (they never grow up you know)"

The mute successful freaks
Fold up their ticking
Droop and trudge away

Then she reveals the feature
That best fits her for this job—
The word NO
That NO of jutted jaw
That stuck her in the employment office window.

The agent looks toward his canvas door,

Can't he see how freaky she is?
Still thinking, of trying, of applying?
Doesn't he know what an attraction she would be
Bound up in Northern Tissue stripes,
Spotting red NOs on his sawdust floor,
Still flowing and she's survived it all?

The agent snaps,
"I don't know
what makes you think you qualify
to be a freak!"
and wheeling,
he enters his one-ring circus,
and closes his ticking door.

TO MY NEXT HUSBAND

Pecan trees grow
Clear into the sky
You reserve for kites,
And even your yard is
Choked with old plantings.

Still, I want to buy you
a pecan tree
And bake you chewy pies,
Sticking myself to your teeth.

BUTTERBALL

Dressed in her old cooking muu muu
Mimi washes her bird like a baby
placed in the kitchen sink spreading
a pale ivory film over his bulging breast
and humming slides her fingers deep
down the curve of his back rolling him over
and crooking her finger
she nudges her glasses
up over her brow and
peers at his pinfeathers.

Pursing her lips she pinches his
blemishes out and rolling him back
rubs his drumsticks tracing the end bones
and rinses his body crooning over the water
you'll be the best bird ever
and huffing and puffing lifts him up on his tail
and taking the flour sack towel
from her shoulder she pats him
thoroughly dry.

PROFESSIONAL

Sun on onion half, damp sacrifice.
carbon blade executes white rainbows
that fall to board/bred to lie
flat and take it without a tear.

GAMBIT

Firmer than my dream
His damp cheek
Presses mine, asleep
On Sunday morning.

His freshly shaven question
Slips into my ear.

BODYSMITHING

I tendril sun browned legs
Around his silver body,
Silhouetting myself
Against his ancient armor.

In this small smelter
His fingers open
spiky with silver
His legs shine white
and bend around my core
Like moonbeams reaching
The other side of the sun.

SHOPPING SPREE

"May I help you, Sir?"
her blue eyes asked.

My own gone green, I watched
You pick three pairs of charcoal slacks,
Five button-down white shirts
    And after hearing her incredulous
    Reply to your remark that you
    Wear only black knit ties,
You bought four colored ones
With covert gusto.

IN GRATITUDE THURSDAY

Remove organs
scrub dead skin
with salt
inside hollow ribs
outside pimpled flesh

Chop chop
peeled white layers
green crescent moons
spill over leafy parsons
and mushrooms
chopped up too.

Add our daily crumbs
sagely spiced to mask
refinement internalized
bathe with broth and dress.

A turkey bought your life of holidays
cooking turkeys.

Stuff it.

MEMENTO

Your white china mug of soap is missing
Along with your stalk of badger bristles.

The naked bathroom sink remains,
Furry with old cut whiskers.

CULINARY SPECULATIONS

If pie in the sky is the moon,
Is it coconut beaches littered with pebbles?
Is it lemon lake clouded with cumulus?
Is it rising romance before the meringue weeps?

FAMILY GAME

Finally a quiet
In the late and foggy morning.

No warm wet morsels crying out from cradles
In primal pain demanding comfort.

No husbands foaming white shirts at the mouth
To stand before me, ironing echoes.

No fried egg eyes witness the body's rhythms
Synchronized to sizzles from the stove.

No apples packed in plain brown lunch bags
Encircling ancient questions at the core.

Finally a quiet
In the late and foggy morning
The only sound around me
Central heating feebly roaring
From the vent hole in the basement.

EARTHMOTHERS RISING

We broke out of single cells,
burrowed up from earthwork spaces,
waited to jump into empty slots
in the revolving doors.
We brought chairs to the table
and came to play his game.

More of us working in rooms together
clustering up under ceilings,
pressing our backs to the roof,
cracking but not breaking the glass.

More of us earning than ever before
79 cents now of each daddy's dollar.

And as we are learning the sense
of the dollar, who is watching our babies?

Who is touching our children
while we drive new on-ramps?

Who is sitting our kids as we slip
into hierarchies massing the sky?

Is it the mother still too bound
by her own body's babies
to mount the ramp of the freeway?

Is it the Psychology Senior majoring
in observing toddlers, his heart in his head
and his head in his wallet?

Woman Song

Is it the display screen of many colors
arcing across the young rainbow brains and
into what banded orders do the colors rise and fall?

Who is raising our children?
Can we trust them to fill in the spaces our rising is shaping?

And where are the daddies
now that it's their turn to come down to earth.

IN THE DAYS BEFORE GLASS CEILINGS

Those husband-men they owe us
all those years working late,
all those mornings leaving early
while we mopped floors with muscles
we dared not use to spread them
those husband-men, to pour them
thin,
like hot wax
over the shining linoleum,
reflecting our cracked
glass slippers.

SERVICE STATION

Yes!
We sisters
Wish to cruise in
Also and pay so cheap
A price as dollars
Instead of souls or psyches
Or hours sweeping floors.

We wish the unfettered freedom of tossing coin,
Presenting body, withholding heart,
And--pleasure softened--to cruise out
The door of his place,
Without a backward
Or beholden glance.

CHIAROSCURO

Thin black
Vivian Eliot
Eyes smudged
Under a glowing
Celluloid brim
Flickered in the
Dark room, speaking
Easily of her brittle
Inevitable death
Across these silent
and
Good night years.

PRIDE

When she was young
she used to pick
more Texas cotton in a day
than any man in the fields,
she bragged with a black cackle.

And once she killed a man in a barroom fight
so her husband, he never messed around on her
No Sir.

She grinned black and white spaces
satisfied
waiting
for him to pick her up
from nine hours
waxing floors and
watching children
at a dollar for each hour
slaved away.

From the 1970s when some white women went to work at minimum wage and hired black housekeepers to watch the children and clean house at even less money.

FRIENDS

When I'm at my words,
My companion's a spider
Suspended in a wispy web
I'm too busy to destroy.

My paper rolling in salutes
That momma long legs hanging
     Motionless motionless
In the thin spun cloud
She strung from desk to drape.

I puff a tiny breath her way—
Poof! She drops behind the desk,
I go on typing.

When next I check her web,
She's back in place—
     Motionless motionless
Having ascended unseen by me,
Too busy at my words.

FOR SELECTRIC EARS

And now there is nothing but
Your modern humming and plastic
Keys—antiphony to the upright's
Ivories I resisted pressing
When soft summer baseball sang out
Cries of companions in the twilight
Street—the team has narrowed to one
Player who popped all the champagne
Bubbles and sold himself to a higher
Bidder, leaving a shrine of shattered
Wineglasses in the cold fireplace.

Now there is nothing but your humming keys
I run to, I run to, I run to.

STUFFED

I'm stuffed, sitting in this brown leather chair
After Max's chocolate éclair, crammed
with vanilla custard, mild and rich
stuffed into the choux, like me stuffed into this
chocolate brown chair.

SOFA TRAP

Frisé of wool gathering mass,
Yesterday's overstuffed life
Positions a me
Too heavy to move.

EXISTENTIAL ANXIETY

She picks
At fingertips
Peels away shreds

Of calloused skin
Exposing tiny patches
Of red flesh

That scab
for her to pick
away again.

BEGIN AGAIN

I am a middle aged graduate
A Bachelor of Arts at last

Twenty years of chopping and stacking
Preparing this forest for inspection
Hardback, paperback, scribbles and scratches
I am the lone librarian of my mind
And her wood pulp extremities;
A Dewey decimal system of the self.

Choose now:
Which shelf for heartwood theories
Hiding behind descriptions flying
Leaves of bright green facts?
Which niche for whispered stories
Scooped from tunnels of blood
And stillness between the covers?

Bachelor of Arts.
Bachelor. Spinster, arts and crafts.
Bachelor of arts
Spinster of craft
Spinner of wool
Weaver of yarns
Woman of dreams undreamt

Bachelor of Arts.
B. A.
Begin. Again.

Summer of 1978

READING MATTER

The skin of my face
Remains folded up
In the mornings
Like yesterday's
Newspapers—
A millions stories
Between the dated lines.

SOLITARY

Anna alone in her room's grey haze
Rolled up one blind and
Let the framed black view
Rub its hand over her cool skin.

The kitchen stove clock's grind
Sounded behind Frigidaire's slumbers
And starts, slumbers and starts.
No one heard Anna breathe out or breathe in.

LABELS

My shopping cart rolls by
Walls of colored paper wrappers
I try to picture the peach halves
Hiding in tiny tin drums.

And grandma steps up from the cellar
Hugging quart jars to her full length apron.

Her peach halves needed no labels
Their shining cup backs stacked
Like fat orange sea turtles
Preserved in an ocean of glass.

SOLSTICES

Yesterday I bought California Blood
Oranges to douse my belly full of fire.
Today I get out the good silver to feed
my children orange blossom soup.
Tomorrow I will say take, eat,
use the sterling I polished for you.

I won't tell them of standing at the sink
pouring thick cream into the advi-
sedly soft white cloth, nor of pressing
this damp pad hard against the bowls
and deep carved shanks of spoons
without base metal, neither of letting
go the cloth to squeeze the forks
between my fingertips, printing
my pattern deep into dumb heirlooms.

Especially I won't say when it is over
that I sniffed my own tarnished fingers
while underneath it all the last warm red
worm crawled out to settle into its own
advisedly soft white cloth.

THE COMING DUST

ONE

I snipped off the last seven lemons hanging from the little tree just outside my kitchen window, the one that faces east. The sun should have come up there each morning, but on stormy days I could only count on lemons, dangling as globes of sunshine through the winter of my husband's diabetes darkness. An amputee now, he sits in his wheelchair, so I bend down to kiss him.

With the lemons all squeezed into hot lemonade and swallowed to ward off colds, I prayed for warmth outside my window.

The last of the lemons had clung for life on their twigs just before I snipped them off, to divert sap to the new life. Spring rains will bring pale green bumps, tight lemon buds, purple in their grip on youth, fearful to unfurl, blossom and die into lemons. The little tree will become blowsy with sour fruit, drooping in her cyclic wisdom.

TWO

Rain gods penetrate the earth, knocking at smooth hard bulbs, knocking to titillate the white root, to feed the green stalk shooting up the pale swelling yellow round head, spiked with sun flares rounding his circumference. The noble jonquil stands proud in the sun, then bends under a downpour, bows to the source of life. Water brings all things clean and green.

Honor will have his day, sparkle and shine, before collapsing into the coming dust.

SHAMELESS HUSSY LOOKS BACK

ONE
After he wheeled his chair in, all independent like
from his morning shower just the other day
and transferred smoothly onto the king-sized bed,
I finished toweling him off and rubbed it dry,
fluffing up the curly golden short hairs it nested in,
Resplendent in its pinky glow.

"No gray hairs down here!" I marveled,
bending over my mate of 29 years
to rub my face lightly back and forth
on his sweet soft sausage,
rolling it around
beneath my lips.

TWO
Back when we were new—
He in his black leather boots, and
I in my shameless hussy moans—
He would have sprung up tall and hard so fast
I couldn't have finished the toweling off
Before he put to use that splendid package,
With his bull balls slung low,
And banging gently on my bum.

I would cling to his skin
And ride him up the steep sides
Of the mountain, onto the high plateau,
Leaving my mind behind
In the merciful death of thoughts,
Simply flying his horse of many colors
Across the vast and lasting mesa.

THREE
After Each of his blood sugar dramas
Like a five-way coronary bypass,
Two carotid artery surgeries,
Claudication of the legs
And Losing a toe here and there
he resumed his relentless and leather-booted interest,
Although Requiring some modifications, some assistance from those little blue pills and from those brown packages that arrived in the mail with various humming and buzzing adult toys he wanted to try out
"I'll never quit," he vowed and indeed
 each time he rose again in bed, triumphant.

My libido shriveled
as spontaneous flights across the highland mesa
Faded into movies in my memory,
And it turned into an unexpected duty to search
To find my shameless hussy's eager heart.

FOUR
"I am still interested," he says today,
but that soft pink sausage resting like a newborn's
 tells a different story
"Did you think I would give up?

I had lately come to hope exactly that
this year since his near death, two-month stay
 in ICU with kidney failure and dialysis,
open wound dressings, and half year of physical therapy
 since the amputation of his left leg, above the knee,

"I sent away for a book on sex for the disabled,"
he says, "but it hasn't arrived yet."

Woman Song

One day soon, the mail will come—
I'm digging deep into the great divide of time
to my shameless hussy long-departed self:

—Come back, come back, come back!

I cry out to her.

—I can't do this all alone!

--Summer of 2008

@Online Dating

My daughter, contented
and single for years
came to a time
that was right,
cast her line into
Plenty of Fish,
and reeled in the one
who didn't get away.

My granddaughter, contented
and single for months
came to a time
that was good,
swiped right and
matched up
with a keeper
on tinder.com

I'm starting to ask myself
is the time's right for looking @ sites
like okCupid,
eHarmony and
silversingles.com

and wondering

Who's out there?

SUNSET SONG

The sun blasts
Her dying reflection
Dark red against the trees
In my small Auburn forest.

She's calling to us
Remember this day
This one day that God
Made for you among so
Many others, this one is
The only one you will ever
Have.

WOMAN SONG MUSIC

I've written poems and stories for years but have only written one song, which then ironically was incorporated into a sculpture by my husband. I was lucky enough to take lessons from the musical genius Hannah Jane Kile, to whom I bow in thanks for setting chords to my song.

E
And she had a little mocha

heart shaped birthmark,

E7
nestled in the curve of her

A
calf, and she noticed he never

E
noticed, and she

B7
loved it just the

E
same.

To hear the song, its rhythms and how it works with the other verses, visit my youtube chanel.

https://www.youtube.com/channel/UC6gYskQ5ZK6vnF4-TSJ3GAA/featured

ABOUT THE AUTHOR

Poet and novelist June Gillam loves writing and writers. She's been published in various venues, most recently in the 2015 issue of *Peregrine*, the literary journal of Amherst Writers & Artists.

In May 2016, June earned a Certificate in Stanford's Online Novel Writing program, in which she focused on the third book in her Hillary Broome novel series, *House of Eire*, set mainly in Ireland. In this series, June explores social issues through characters wounded by powerful cultural forces.

After completing a master's degree in English, Creative Writing Emphasis, with The Dream Malfunctions poetry collection as a culminating project, June earned a Ph.D. in Transformative Learning and Change. Her dissertation was published by Lambert Academic Publishing under the title *Creating Juicy Tales: Cooperative Inquiry into Writing Stories*. That work forms the foundation of *Writing in Small Groups the 4color Way*, published by Gorilla Girl Ink.

She has taught various English courses at Cal State Sacramento, American River College and San Joaquin Delta College, where she pioneered online writing classes in 1998, for which she was honored as a Distinguished Faculty Member.

Her indie press Gorilla Girl Ink publishes most of her books, and she is working with a young author known as Mud, who writes paranormal adventure. His first title, *The Raven's Nest*, is available now and will be followed by other coming of age tales. Gorilla Girl Ink plans to offer the works of other writers in the future.

June's research subject interests include the inner dynamics of writing and those of writing support groups. She is a founding member of the San Joaquin Valley Writers branch of the California Writers Club and was honored to receive their Jack London Award in 2017. She is happy to chat with writers who post Reply Comments in her blog at www.junegillam.com where her titles can be purchased.

Follow her on twitter @junegillam
and Instagram at jgillam700
and https://www.facebook.com/GorillaGirlInk/
and http://gorillagirlpress.com/

If you enjoyed this book, June would greatly appreciate even a one or two line review on Amazon or Goodreads. If you would like to talk over anything writing related, please email her at gorillagirlink@gmail.com

Other books by June Gillam
Available at amazon.com and B&N.com and elsewhere

Poetry. *So Sweet Against Your Teeth: Poems from Childhood's Fall.* "Gillam speaks to the confusion and mixed signals of everyone's childhood, and the ultimate acceptance of yourself, scars and all." - Excerpt from amazon review

Social Issues Suspense Novels: Hillary Broome Series

House of Cuts. "[T]his is a genuine narrative of the plights of many American families across the country who have been affected by the infiltration of Big-Box stores that have ultimately been the demise of small mom and pop shops." -Excerpt from amazon review

House of Dads. " Women Cannot Run the Show? We'll See Grandpa!" -Excerpt from amazon review

House of Eire. "[C]omplex characters and carefully rendered settings, the result of years of careful introspection, observation and reflection." -Excerpt from amazon review

House of Hoops. Hillary, an old curmudgeon called Charlie and Hillary's daughter Claire confront one another in a Northern California basketball and urban development setting. To be released in 2019.

How to: *Writing in Small Groups the 4color Way*

Contact June if you would like to start a Cooperative Inquiry small group focused on writing.

Other books published by Gorilla Girl Ink

Paranormal Adventure: *The Raven's Nest* by MUD

Watch gorillagirlpress.com for upcoming new releases.

End Note: In some of the print versions of Woman Song, there is a format oddity. Readers who spot this may email me and receive a prize for their eagle eyes. gorillagirlink@gmail.com

www.ingramcontent.com/pod-product-compliance
Lightning Source LLC
Chambersburg PA
CBHW050607300426
44112CB00013B/2118